Thousand-Cricket Song

*For Joanne ~
With appreciation ~
Catherine*

Thousand-Cricket Song

Catherine Strisik

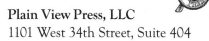

Plain View Press, LLC
1101 West 34th Street, Suite 404

www.plainviewpress.net
Austin, TX 78705

ISBN: 978-1-63210-025-2
Second Edition, 2016, published by Plain View Press.

Library of Congress Number: 2009942173

Cover photograph: *Tuol Sleng Prison,* by Larry Schreiber
Interior photographs by Catherine Strisik
Author photo: Jim O'Donnell, Taos, New Mexico

to Michael Schreiber (Chhouet),

U Sam Oeur,

and Ouk Damry,

survivors

Acknowledgments

Grateful acknowledgment is made to the following publications in which these poems first appeared or are forthcoming, sometimes in alternate forms.

"A Buffet After Genocide," *Canteen 6*, 2010;

"Marketplace in Siem Reap," "Humidity," *Chokecherries Anthology*, 2007;

"Shade," "Twenty-Four Years After the Refugee Camp, A Reunion," *Fogged Clarity*, November 2009;

"Khmer Orphan, American Girl and Her Red Bandana,"*42opus Volume 8 #1*, March 2008;

"On Course to Snake Island," *House Organ #64*, Fall 2008;

"From All That We Heard" *Sin Fronteras/Writers Without Borders Journal #13*, April 2009;

"Body Guard," "Festival of the Reversing Current," *Studio* Vol.4 No. 1 2010;

"Tuol Sleng Prison," "Buton's Wife," "Our Positions Along the Mekong," "The Woman at Pol Pot's Grave," "Roadside Temple Dissonance," "In the Twenty-First Century," "Place Setting," *Southwest Literary Center* 2006 Anthology, (chosen for the New Mexico Discovery Award), December 2006;

"Land Mine," *War, Literature, and the Arts*, 2009.

Gratitude

My sincerest gratitude to the Vermont Studio Center from where this manuscript was begun, and the Colrain Manuscript Conference from where it was shaped and nearly finished. I offer my heartfelt appreciation to my long-time Taos writing group and friends who have encouraged every step of the way before and after: Judith Hovetter, Kayce Verde, Morgan Farley, and to Jamie Ross, kindred spirit, for his insight and extraordinary talent. To Alexander Long, for igniting the flame, and the perceptive eye and careful readings of John Nichols, Veronica Golos and Rebecca Dyer, and my mother, Nancy Strisik who read every word and believed.

I am deeply indebted to U Sam Oeur and Ken McCullough who came into my life well into this project to support, clarify, encourage, question, keeping me immersed so that I would not forget, and so that others will not forget either.

And finally, to Larry and Dimitra Schreiber, my beloveds, who with me, witnessed Cambodia, thank you for waiting, listening and hearing.

Contents

II.

A dog that has nowhere to go;
Waves that cannot go beyond the bank

III.

*I see that it is the rainy season and most of Cambodia
is submerged in silver, shimmering water.*

Because The River Suffers All That She Adores

from Dawn Along the Tonle Sap

There are layers to Catherine Strisik's *Thousand-Cricket Song*, as there are layers to everything and everyone in Cambodia. What you see is not often what you get, as in the poem "Boat Ride," in which the poet witnesses an apparent suicide by drowning to which everyone, except the poet, is indifferent. Interpretation is in the eye of the beholder; one must understand the context. The beholder in these poems keeps a discerning eye. When confronting what happened during Pol Pot, for example, it is hard not to vent one's rage in paroxysms of self-righteousness, but Strisik maintains a remarkable balance between subjectivity and objectivity as she makes this journey. There are wonderful lyric pieces such as "One American Girl and Her Khmer Sister" and "On Course to Snake Island" juxtaposed with stark reportage, as in "Roadside Temple Dissonance," "Fortune," and "Fifteen-Year Old Khmer Rouge Soldier." Some poems, such as "From All That We Heard" combine both. This is in keeping with Cambodia, a place of incredible beauty yet profound corruption and certainly a haunted history in recent years.

One might also be tempted to penetrate the "heart of darkness" in Cambodia by adopting the persona of Pol Pot or Ta Mok, let's say, but Strisik chooses, instead, to show us "The Woman at Pol Pot's Grave" –a portrait of a woman who still believes in Pol Pot and tends the site of his cremation. Strisik, wisely, presents us with the paradigm in its own terms. There are even several poems of comic relief, "Sacrificial Pig" being the most notable. The weave of the tableau is seamless, transparent when it needs to be, opaque when it must be. The visceral realities of life abound—urine-stained feet, a miscarriage, flies, prostitution—but the blitheness of the spirit abides.

Half the poems in the book focus on women, childbearing and childbirth. These poems could easily be placed side by side and presented as a powerful choral piece in which we experience, by increments, the poet's deepening understanding, hence solidarity.

While the cumulative effect is of limitlessness, Strisik eschews hyperbole; she merely shifts to a wider and higher angle. "Body Guard" is the stunning fulcrum of this suite.

Strisik recognizes and admits to being an outsider, that her consciousness and the consciousness of Cambodia are not the same. The poem "Fortune" contains these lines:

> hand-held mirror,
> its crack of recognition
> between our cultures…

The poet is pulled between her own sensibility and sensuality and that on the other side of the mirror. Poems such as "Seeing Hands," "Our Positions Along the Mekong," and "Reflecting Pond at Angkor Wat" present poignant examples of this. One recalls Forster's *Passage to India* among many other works in which a character confronts this otherness and is undone. But Strisik's vision penetrates the surfaces and she accepts what she finds. Kipling said "Oh, East is East and West is West, and never the twain shall meet." Catherine Strisik shows us that if we locate the center and are still, we can apprehend the moment, as well as witness the flow in which that moment is carried, whether it be East or West.

The book ends fittingly with "Festival of the Reversing Current." These are the final lines of the poem:

> The old vast water, forceful and
> god-like in its autumnal appearance sweeps
>
> into the waiting estuaries
> of their hearts
> first to clean, then to harvest.
>
> Who would not walk this
> walk, this dutiful gesture
> on naked feet, the unmistakable
>
> dancing late into each night.

One must understand the Mekong (and the Tonle Sap) to understand the systole and diastole of Cambodian life. Tonle Sap Lake is the heart of the organism that is Cambodia, literally. During the monsoon season the tide reverses and the water flows up the Mekong and Tonle Sap Rivers to increase the size of Tonle Sap Lake from 2,700 square km to 16,000 km. *Thousand-Cricket Song* is infused with this awareness, on a cellular level. Catherine Strisik intuits the soul of the apsara and absorbs the primal rhythms of this haunting place without losing herself.

The poems in this book are well-wrought, including the repetition of certain words threaded through the poems like beads. There is a tendency, when speaking of recent Cambodian history, to cite the entirety of that history and of Cambodian culture, not to show that you know it, but to make sure the reader is grounded in the context. Many will be, many won't—some will be jolted awake by the knowledge that any of this ever happened during their lifetimes, despite more recent instances such as Rwanda and Darfur. Strisik chooses to limit her references, and trust our intelligence as readers.

Thousand-Cricket Song is lithe, articulate, lively and perceptive. Strisik is a skilled poet, with a clear and uncluttered voice. The life force of Cambodia has passed into her and galvanized her poems.

Ken McCullough, Winona, MN

Ken McCullough is the author of numerous books of poetry and fiction, as well as co-translator of U Sam Oeur's *Sacred Vows* and co-author of U's memoir *Crossing Three Wildernesses.*

I.

Tuol Sleng: Hill of the Poison Tree

Cambodian women at Angkor Wat Temple

Tuol Sleng Prison

Please say each skull has a voice
and an appetite. When I press
my ear to their jaws, crab

shells and dried rice drop out.
Then their smells rise to me:
lemon grass, coriander,

mint leaves. Now empty
their sustenance. Disquieted
their once envied salts

and palm sugar. Please say
each skull has a voice. What can I do
with you, my sound, their tongues' undressing.

In the Nail Salon, Siem Reap

My feet have no history here.
Not once have my soles been beaten, toenails
pulled, yet I keep company with the girls
who squat here on the warm dirt.

The woman in the one salon chair goes
gradually hairless: even fine facial hair
is shaved with the unsanitary blade.

I have no say in her dream.
I am without resemblance to the Khmer.
My feet are American, their so-white

prettiness urine-stained
by my own aimlessness.
I cannot scrub hard enough.

The woman admires her shaved face
in the hand-held mirror, beams
as the toenails on her bruised feet
are polished burgundy.

A Buffet After Genocide

The mood might have been the same as now —
miniature birds and red chili,
stuffed thin pancakes and grilled octopus on Ochheuteal Beach.
The quiet atmosphere of hot, phantom faces

in the shadow of a shiny Land Rover,
in the warmth of the sand in Sihanoukville,
where the men rest in hammocks,
and the body's silence begins to blister,

the Khmer children run from the tide in the gulf,
the foreign woman swims topless,
all of us unexpectedly laughing —
Even the bodyguard sitting on the bench

      with his pistol,
inhaling smoke from his cigarette,
sunglasses removed.

Dawn Along the Tonle Sap

for Syna Sim

And her guttural sound at dawn breaks the water's surface,
shoulders cool and wrapped in a pashmina of silk,
which warms and flutters as she ponders.

Outside her, Phnom Penh lies slow in motion and she
stands aware in the short shadow of meager flesh.
And the sun rises. Its rays upon her body

are both urgent and affectionate, and pull
the woman close to the river's edge. She cries out
to her newborn without response—

And when the current embraces,
it weeps this name —

because the river suffers all that she adores.

Boat Ride

We rode along the Tonle Sap River in a boat in the morning.
Fishing nets spread across the water's surface.

Suddenly a man jumped out of his small fishing boat into the river.
Our friend motioned with his hands for us to look

the other way.
We moved rapidly north.

Mosquito nets and hammocks hung from shacks on the shore.
We looked back and saw no one helping the man

who by this time bobbed up and down in the river
then was gone.

Our friend appeared unmoved and looked forward.
His lips pressed tight.

From All That We Heard

What remained was only that orphan running
barefoot through rice paddies — not what she sang,
not even the pimp waving his hands full of riel.
Only the sound of her feet sloshing along the riverbed
and in the dank hall of the magnificent temple
of the white-robed Buddha which now, defaced,
daunts the praying for moments —
the sound of the running and the sound of the gunfire.

Land Mine

As if it could help I dropped a riel in his bucket at Ta Prohm —

invisible, eyes birthwet

inside the shade.

His drum's hide, worn — a water buffalo

    returned
    to the rice paddy before evening —

    hearts surely split
    by the unexpected thunder.

Rida

So small and with such small feet, I watch
my own. She reminds me of my own

absent childhood, the dead
and their worn crucifixes. Yet, she is young

with adorned sandals on her dusty feet.
Oh, mana mou

The water reverses
upstream to the mouth

of the Tonle Sap River, and beyond,
the Tonle Sap Lake. Listen. Her eyes

embrace mine with an aching recognition.
All thought halts. Only the flow.

Fifteen-Year-Old Khmer Rouge Soldier

shoves the bayonet blade into the pleading
mother's vagina. The blade

stops short
at the pubic bone, for a moment

a difficult position.
Yanks out the blade,

for a moment, stands back, watches
the throb and bleed, slices

through the pregnant abdomen,
pulls out the fetus

with a bare hand. Hangs it
from the line pulled taut

between two trees in a forest
with the others

already blackened from the days' sun.

Body Guard

When the baby came
it came in pieces: skull dropped
onto dirt where chickens scratch, limbs
fell between porcelain footsteps.
I recognized my daughter's face
in its face. I covered it with a rag.

When the baby came, I tossed
the brain stem over the wall
of the tin outhouse. I drowned it
in the seashore next to Khmer girls
selling octopus skewers. I rubbed it
against my inner thighs. I named it Helen.

The bodyguard waited with a thin tissue,
handed it to me. I did not know what to do
with the tissue: wipe blood off my foot?
Wipe away another tear?
Life begins with lovemaking
and ends. I smudged her
onto my husband's palm.

Tunnel

So when the Khmer mother spread her
weak thighs just once

was enough, under
the weight of October's humidity,

she tried for an instant to hear
the dear whimper, the unbroken heart

but in the moment's lull and bareness
her baby had already stopped breathing.

Too sad even to respond
between her bloodline and her spirit

cry why she felt relieved
from this body's thin

sound, those
pierced on her name-sake —

cell, glory, and all
that lightweight silence.

She was winter now
within the ruined tunnel, her utter

barrenness, her unlikely voice
longingly gesturing

Oh, Oh

This day ends in quiet preparation
for sleep.

As though rebirth were tomorrow
for the baby she so loved,

the draft inside
fragrant newborn.

Place Setting

The table is set with bone china, sautéed
miniature birds. We eat.
Our host's wife laughs often — listen

respond and nod —
In the kitchen the help squats around a boiling pot.
The cook looks up from her bowl, smiles

as we pass the doorway — such a simple
rural gesture that I, too, would like to squat
around the boiling pot, and sip.

No division. No place setting.
To be oddly out-of-place in Cambodia.
Not to be "only you" but "you too."

Steaming broth, another point of view, easily seen.
Our daughter responds, twists
her silk button between her fingers

or squats around that boiling pot, close to the cook.

One American Girl and Her Khmer Sister

Each has their secret view and if left
alone with one another might say
some words, however narrow,
about the sky during and after a monsoon,
the dark in the center of their rivers;
Tonle Sap and Rio Grande, the doll,
who dresses herself for the river expedition
in the so blue silk shift.
The secret pale as the lens.
The ripe cherries dripping from the cherry tree.

Secrets of the Khmer Farmer

His palms press against his cheeks,
and squeeze out a little pain
onto the river's surface,

a little nakedness. And he sees
rice paddies and the rice paddies cup
his light body ashamed

the way a thin soul bruises
in the mid-day sun. And his hands, scarred
all over, left sorrow on either shore exhausted

by fear, sanity impaired, the wonder
too frail. A cry from his waste
where their hair still flows.

What We Did Not Know Until Now

Say, I love my husband who lies next to me,
how I caught him in the upper corner
of the photograph, not wearing the krama,
rather the other men who stood close by
as if with broken skulls
and the kramas wrapped tight around their faces,
held in something,
held in the world
that we touched with our palms
sweating.

II.

A dog that has nowhere to go:

Waves that cannot go beyond the bank

Cambodian Proverb

Bas-Relief of celestial dancers "apsaras" on a
wall at Angkor Wat Temple

Shade

The famous Khmer artist has placed his palm
on a murderer's upper back near the neck, has pushed him

toward the painting on the prison museum's wall.
Outside the perimeter the mother is mute on her knees.

Her hands cradle a beautiful fatigue
as if she had just remembered why:

a bayonet blade held upright
to catch an infant as it spins through the air.

The shade shades the body this evening
in Phnom Penh.

He cleans his brushes alone each day
in the medicinal turpentine, wipes

his palette clean, and becomes silent.
The painting is his settlement with humiliation.

You can hear the crickets' trill in the banyans.
You can hear the whole evening is crying louder.

The New Holy Medicine

They had tried monks' blessings,
Chinese cures, and faith healers.
They had tried herbal remedies
and home altars for praying.
They had blackouts, convulsions.
They had nightmares.
They had all the karma they could take.

The Breaking

Ride all afternoon in a tuk tuk off Sisowath Quay, off
Monivong Boulevard behind the country truck that's

just entered the city from National Route 1. Notice
the eyes peering out from the slats

along the sides of the truck. Witness the nuances
of innocence and the strain in the lines of a woman. See

not only the wicker baskets with live pigs grunting
inside and the bicycles and luggage piled high. Reflect her

lack of expression between the chickens and the ducks clucking
and quacking. She prays to Buddha and almost

sleeps on her feet while the slats' shadows lengthen
against her cheeks. Imagine only quiet, and beyond that, her gaze

back at you while the tightly woven baskets with fruits
and vegetables for Phnom Penh's markets are unloaded. Become

undone by her smile, by the unbearable humidity and the sky's
hazy white. Watch her yawn and her sarong shift below her waist.

She moves to the ground and you smell garlic cloves,
ginseng and the heat flows from her because the breaking

can no longer be bodied again.

Roadside Temple Dissonance

I want
to understand   devotees
who pray   at the roadside temple
not standing necessarily
    still
because the chimes will not allow for stillness.

Their desire is to be
silent   to combine   absolute wholeness
and the isolated cuts
they fear.

How to believe
in Buddha's meditative stance?
The reflection.   The party
is only pretend
now, the boiled prawns and grilled octopus.
Geckos continue to eye everyone from their positions
on the wall.

Enough?
How do the devotees refuse to feel
their country's split
belly. The suffocating incense.
The chimes carry discord
through the air, greedy,
disillusioned.

Marketplace in Siem Reap

A girl points to the fattest hanging pig. Cut
from its delicate hook, the seller binds
the body in a rag she pulls from her cloth sack.
Along the river front, the thin and thirsty
gather. A one-legged beggar holds
out his hands. A barefoot mother pushes
her baby's face against the cab window.
As the girl moves to gather greens from baskets
pig juices stain its wrap. I worry
about the meat, the small movement inside.
A yellow blouse, Cambodian silk, hangs
its question among unrefrigerated meats that drop
from their claws and crooked necks, torsos hooked
to braided ropes looped from rafters.
Light reflects from the spirit.

Night Pool

The foreign man gestured to the young girl, and hoped
he'd be the groom. He spoke French until the sun

set's rays bleached the air and floated on the water
with a basket of longans. As the young girl's

faith numbed, she envisioned the foreign man
with the other girls outside these gardened walls—

liquid eyeliner, braless breasts, many small apsaras
laid out to pierce, and all mothers, beggar thin.

.

Fortune

Born pretty in Cambodia, she suffers
her father and older brothers
as they drug then carry her
often without underwear
to the roadside in late afternoon.

She is the virgin living the legend
as the cure for AIDS and hunger.

For one week I see her
young hands reach for the Khmer
who leaves her to be paid for
by foreign men.

Two years later, I think of her
hand-held mirror,
its crack of recognition
between our cultures. *Pretty*.

American Girl Doll

Because the girl stepped forward

carrying her doll, because

her hair fell to her waist

and swung when she moved

because the guard could not see her face

he reached out his hand to touch her hair.

The girl blinked. The guard's longing faded

in the doll's long blank stare.

Our Positions Along the Mekong

At sunrise a woman, her Achilles' stretched, squats
at the river's edge close to my hotel room,
smiling and smiling some teeth.
What does she hear from its movement at 5 a.m.?
What does she hear from constancy and luck's flow?
Does she consider the fish, her birthright swimming by?
The survival of a woman in that instance
her position as flow,
is silent, and not random.

What she sees pulses
and what she doesn't see is not meant to last.

I want to tell her to stand up now.

I want to tell her to straighten her memorized spine
curled into position for survival.
She sips from a communal tin cup,
the others waiting their turn. Her laughter
is like her spine   slightly

dignified and blue. But her smile penetrates
precisely through the poor morning.

What she sees forgives
and what she doesn't see cannot be touched.

I want to tell her to stand up now.

The Prayer

I jab jackfruit, lychee
bananas with burning
incense at this altar
without windows, broken
Buddha shifts the lotus
position gratified.

Humidity

Children sweat in the humidity.
Sausages hang out to dry.
One-legged Nara limps up to say
that the whir of the cicadas
burns the night.
Each elephant walking by
hangs its head.
Silver fish ferment into sauce.
One-legged Nara takes us
to the woman selling captured birds
where we abandon dusty overgrowth.

Reflecting Pond at Angkor Wat

At Mount Meru   one monk
dressed in orange robes   a slow, driftlike
masturbation down ninety laterite steps.

I'm told November is the cool season.

His eyes sift the eight directions.
I stand in the fourth, to the west.

Even Khmer site-seers sigh, shade their faces
from the mid-afternoon sun.

He carries a black bound book.

I listen to at least five languages, can't
understand a word.

Vishnu appears in the tower—
rises out endless wing beats against the sky.
The monk as monk glances back, notices
the extended sapphire appearance.

Our fate here is under control.

He makes his monk's life difficult for himself, descending upon me.
Within minutes I am his
next lover.

Your hair is very pretty, he reads from his book.

We sweat
in the Gallery of a Thousand Buddhas.

The monk as male stands close, brushes a forearm against my breast,
as if by accident. I notice
his eyes, now how they will not look at mine.

There is a question:
How to be obedient in a monk's robe?

In this temple
pleasure is practiced from every angle.
For now, his shy and clever pleasure is my unwashed American
scent and the breast that nursed one infant.

And mine?

The Reflecting Pond holds Angkor Wat during the final moments.

He knows from practice
the woman always leaves.
It's just a matter of sunset.

I drop two dollars in quarters into his hand.

Cambodia: In the Twenty-First Century

I go to the fishing shacks
at the boatyard to taste
fresh fish, and buy prawns
from the gulf. When I arrive,
riel in hand, I hear a TV.
No fish here.
No fish anywhere.
In every shack, a TV
where the fish are supposed to be.

Sacrificial Pig

Even the pig, fresh meat washed and polished
this November morning, is ready
for its important role in today's ceremony.
If I were the pig I'd furrow

my pink brow at Buddha's clay eyes. I'd leave
my brain by the altar, soul by the gate, pig's feet
and pig nose in a glass jar.
If I were the pig I'd dream

of my sty. I'd ask, "Why me?
What goodness have I displayed
in my life to deserve to lie by Buddha's feet?"
If I were the pig, I'd lick my lips, relax

my tongue, release my jaw, and wait
for a ripe pear. I'd be displayed
at the roadside temple between Phnom Penh
and Kampong Som, so that all who stopped to pray

would think, "Look at that lucky pig."
I'd lie on a sacrificial bed of roses, lit
incense around my flesh.
If I were the pig, I'd be smoked and poked, chewed

and spewed. I'd let you decorate me
with blossoms, candles and musical instruments.
I'd want you to stroke me. I'd want you to welcome
the aching blush and savor

my taste, my sweet spoiled salty blood.

III.

I see that it is the rainy season and most of

Cambodia is submerged in silver, shimmering water.

Loung Ung

Mekong River, Cambodia

On Course to Snake Island

Today the boatman,
beautiful and unswerving, pretends himself
invisible at the helm
of his naga-faced boat.

Its slant
eyes and full lips mirror yours,
my boatman, but you cannot hide
inside the wake
anymore than Shackleton by a voyage
of modest competent sense.

Like a serpent
divine, in the Gulf of Siam's dusk,
to recognize his sea hunger,
I watch among unimagined blue
inaudible ripples, your revealed purpose,
boatman,
poised, solitary.

Inside Cambodia

The holy and the old
women chew betel nut
and weave cloth on looms
in the mid-morning
while the monks gather
alms through their black-
and-blue blessings.

Coming of Age

In the hotel in Siem Reap, daughter sleeps
naked beneath the sheet, and hears
the mother scrape the dirt off her heels
and hears the father's pages turn and we hear
the growth of her molars and the wave of her
hair blow in the late breeze. In the morning
she is not as tired, the night cooled.
Only our armpits are warm.

With Damry at Ta Prohm

For me, he repeats the four
Khmer principles: love, honesty

purity, unselfishness swallowed
by the twisted, gnarled

jungle, their roots' muscular embrace.
His face, a recognizable Khmer hue.

The women wearing hats look up
at the great stone expressions.

He straightens his blouse, lights
another cigarette. The crickets chirp

inside the branches' ruins.
With no breeze, the smoke, a fine halo above us.

In the sky, slowed stars, dim gold,
a rice pot. Across the road children swim

in the water once
meant for royalty, he says.

The Woman at Pol Pot's Grave

She's not in love at all but busy,
plucking his last bone bits
from the cremation site, with reverence,
red mourning string tied around her wrist,
hand caress of all smooth pieces.
It's muddy, so no one can tell
what she's cradling, a phalange,
stapes, or thoracic vertebrae —
her earthwork, hoarding
what the others before her have left
behind, and sometimes, at dusk,
dry cow dung. At the site most mutter
his name while she sells gasoline and
herbaceous plants from her house —funny
almost —the kinship created
between his spirit world and the snake
that slithers out from his ashes.

Buton's Wife

She boiled the broth boiled
the birds for the pretty
party painted scarlet on her
lips for an evening's permanent
smirk. Tore the gizzard

tore the heart that cracked
the crystal with its clover cries.
She held the heart in a cup
as fine as the king's
of the poor country, swaddled

against her breast
in silk and the inexplicable
pulse of wings. She climbed
one hundred stone temples
with one hundred charmed

goddesses in a sun so hot set
the sails where the rivers gather
in innocence−
a gesture's nakedness
at her dining table under the relaxed

mango tree with the delicate cow
and other prized possessions.
She gathered us here as unhurrying
American guests, young bird remains
in our bowls, eyes slightly off,

off-center.

Seeing Hands

I liked his hands there on my body
in the dark. Born blind, he touched
Buddha's robes, he said, the walled apsaras,

his grandmother's withered skin.
Quiet objects. I admit
there was a moment I wanted him

to look at my body already filling
an unnamed shape in its forty-sixth year.
His fingers stroked between

my fleshy thighs the
strands of hair. His breath always close.
He stood beyond my feet, it felt, at least three days,

hazy-eyed, lids half closed,
as if this much time was necessary for him to see
my shadow with his, now his hands, now his eyes.

He stroked my skin the way he knew
best. Perhaps my body felt
unfortunate. As if my core was missing.

I felt my oils wept
through open pores, that his palms never used
any other lubricant than that seepage

from my body.
I kept thinking how, with each stroke,
every essence of him, sectioned me, pearl-white fury,

how in the end I'd ask him for a cigarette, give him all
my swollen sorrow in return.

Flies

What's there not to like
in a country so thick with flies
they swarm my bowl of rice, the same flies
that followed me to the toilet hole in the ground
where I held up my skirt, pulled
down my panties and squatted, then hosed off,
the same flies that landed on my naked ass
as I dripped dry.

Twenty-Four Years After the Refugee Camp, a Reunion

Fireworks explode over the Mekong.

The restaurant balcony is a pop-eyed gecko damp with pity.

Friends drink
a second Ankgor Beer each.

The Khmer puts on his glasses, continuously.
Mind wanders between this world
and the world.

Tonight, the baffled city soothes
itself with curious costumed dancers.

The American doctor's heart grasps for
forgetting and some kind of god

which is like someone
wearing a mask
and holding the shatters

in gloved hands.

Skull Map of Cambodia: Song

I see you are the teacher articulating
Khmer to your elementary

class. And you, the physician who studied
in Bangkok and you, mother-to-be,

beautiful thirsty-mouthed joy stretched
down to your abdomen,

and the bride-to-be, your first and only kiss. You, poet
who appears to walk on the pebbled beach whose

lips hold at "Ode." I see you are the seamstress
who says scissors and silk, and you, grandmother

whose skull's reshaped by the shovel that holds.
You are already weak and so old.

Careful is death's cradle that all your mouths
should remain singing. All hear the tenor,

the sweet orange-voiced soprano. Each mouth
recognized by its concluding song.

Khmer Orphan, American Girl and Her Red Bandana

Say, "remove your red bandana" and even her doll's eyes blink—
even the Mekong stops flowing,
even the small Khmer orphan.
The throw-away camera aims, and shoots
an expression, arm distance away.

Say, "remove your red bandana" again,
and the tambourines shake louder.
The orphan's outstretched voice rises
and pushes past the on-lookers to see.
Say it again,

tossing into the basket one riel then another—
and the orphan steps out of her place to become
another. The Mekong resumes,
sweeps along the banks fascinated
doll wide-eyed.

Pirogue Races

One hundred canoes launch with the full moon and two
painted eyes on the carved prows of the naga heads
carrying forty paddlers each. Some stand, most sit.

Using lacquered ceremonial paddles, the leaders in the prows
beat out the rhythm for the crew while the helmsmen steer
a steady course. The dutiful cheering crowd lines

the Mekong's banks. Some in the moment,
when the most beautifully decorated boat cuts
through the finish line's invisible string, bow

while the milky stork clatters its bill. Their wing noise
and the abundance of freshly hatched fish flow
with the current into the next year's full moon phase.

Light

Mottled Saturday night beauty
on Phnom Penh's boulevard, young
and old faces —
Every time the sun sets beauty
breathes out into the night holds
still for digestion imagines the monsoon's
slant only a few days away the fraying
crowd without their glasses drops
its eyes to the black river searching
for a sun waiting for a grandfather,
as though the water is medicinal and its
halted fluidity.

Mottled beauty. It's quick. It's inviting
and follows with hands held in prayer.
The young boy stops close to the kiosk. Yes, he sees
        the beauty.
His little shirt is red and blue striped. Only his grin
        is a thought his few
        teeth reflecting dusk.

But the faces are not cured of their holes
and shades of humiliation.
They don't hurry along the boulevard don't
notice their own mottled
        beauty some grilled
        prawns to remind —
about the lasting luxuries and the rising water —
the sobs and carrier of   *Oh God*

Festival of the Reversing Current

The moment the river reverses itself
into the mouth of the Tonle Sap Lake
it is the bonzes that return

from the search for their souls.
Monks drifting in their persimmon robes,
and the blood of fertility,

somewhat pale,
everything in motion —
bend to Buddha outside the curtained cloth.

The river flows.
It carries the past, present,
and future, curving through Cambodian

villages, fast and familiar,
its lips full with surrender,
its confidence turning

their heads. Heavenly apsaras
and the storks lost in the foliage,
the village elder sitting high

in the doorway of her stilted house
receiving from the flow
all that is recognizable, greater

than her pallor.
The old vast water, forceful and
god-like in its autumnal appearance sweeps

into the waiting estuaries
of their hearts
first to clean, then to harvest.

Who would not walk this
walk, this dutiful gesture
on naked feet, the unmistakable

dancing late into each night.

Endnotes

1. "Tuol Sleng Prison"(p21)— now known as Tuol Sleng Genocide Museum, in Phnom Penh, capital of Cambodia. The site is a former high school which was used as Security Prison 21 (S21) by the Khmer Rouge regime where between 14,000 to 20,000 people were imprisoned, repeatedly tortured, and killed.

2. "A Buffet After Genocide" (p23)— *Occheuteal Beach*— One of the main beaches in the town of Sihanoukville on the south coast of Cambodia.

3. "From All That We Heard" (p26)— *riel*— currency of Cambodia.

4. "Rida" (p28)— *mana mou*— term of endearment for mother in Greek.

5. "Place Setting" (p33)— *not to be only you but you too*— Yannis Ritsos

6. "What We Did Not Know Until Now" (p36)— *krama*— a colorful checked cotton scarf, almost universally worn by rural Khmers (Cambodians), and in cities to protect against nature's elements. The krama is symbolic of Cambodia and for many Khmers, wearing one is an affirmation of their identity.

7. "Shade" (p41)— from the documentary, "S21: The Khmer Rouge Killing Machine" and a painting by Tuol Sleng prison survivor, Cambodian artist, Van Nath.

8. "The New Holy Medicine" (p42)— Prozac; the psychiatric drug in combination of talk therapy that is currently being used to treat a nation of 12 million traumatized people, the survivors and the children of survivors of the Khmer Rouge's mass killings.

9. "The Breaking" (p43)— Sisowath Quay and Monivong Boulevard— two of the main roadways in capital city, Phnom Penh.

10. "Night Pool" (p46)— *longans*— a native fruit to Southern China now grown in some south Asian areas resembling the eyeball of an oriental dragon.

   apsara— a female spirit of the clouds and water in Hindu and Buddhist mythology; they appear as young women of great beauty and elegance who are proficient in the art of dancing.

11. "Reflecting Pond at Angkor Wat" (p52)— *Mount Meru*— in mythology, the principal temple of Angkor in Cambodia, built as a symbolic representation of Mount Meru.

12. "On Course to Snake Island" (p61)— *naga*— in Southeast Asian mythology, a race of supernatural beings usually depicted with both snake and human attributes; the Naga is revered as the original ancestor of the Cambodian people.

    Shackleton's Voyage— Ernest Shackleton, expedition leader to Antarctica in 1914-15, who survived with his crew at sea 1200 miles away from the nearest outpost of humanity.

13. "Inside Cambodia" (p62)— *betel nut*— native fruit of the Areca catechu palm tree in Southeast Asia that contains the stimulant arecoline, often chewed alone or with lime; frequent use stains teeth black.

    alms— In Buddhism, alms (material offerings) are given by lay people to monks and nuns to nurture virtue, merit and blessings and to ensure monastic continuity.

14. "The Woman at Pol Pot's Grave" (p65)— *Pol Pot* (Saloth Sar) was the leader of the communist movement known as "Khmer Rouge" (Red Khmer), who forced approximately 26% of the Cambodian population between 1975-79 into slave labor, malnutrition, and executions while imposing a version of agrarian collectivization.

15. "Seeing Hands"(p67)— trained blind people in the art of massage in Phnom Penh and Siem Reap.

16. "Twenty-Four Years After the Refuge Camp, A Reunion" (p70)— my husband Larry Schreiber, a physician for the American Red Cross on the Thai/Cambodian border for three months, befriended Ouk Damry, a young survivor who had wandered into the refugee camp.

17. "Skull Map of Cambodia: Song" (p71)— a "map" of Cambodia made from the skulls of victims, showing the Tonle Sap and Mekong Rivers with symbolic blood-red water, displayed at the Tuol Sleng Genocide Museum.

18. "Pirogue Races" (p73)— *pirogue* (pie-rog)— a small, flat-bottomed boat.

19. "Festival of the Reversing Current" (p75)— *bonze*— monk

About the Author

Catherine Strisik, poet and co-editor of the online journal, *Taos Journal of International Poetry & Art* (www.taosjournalofpoetry. com). She is the author of the poetry collection, *The Mistress*: a journey with the intricacies and ravages of Parkinson's Disease and its accompanying betrayals, loves, and acceptances, and the diminishment and enlightenment of both the physical and spiritual self (3: A Taos Press, 2016). Active in the Taos poetry community for over 33 years, her poems appear in *Journal of Feminist Studies in Religion, Drunken Boat, Connotation Press: An Online Artifact, Kaleidoscope,* and elsewhere. Strisik has received grants, honors and prizes from *CutThroat, Peregrine,* and *Comstock Review,* The Southwest Literary Center, The Puffin Foundation, as well as a residency at the Vermont Studio Center. Strisik is also a Dyslexia Language Therapist who practices privately and in Taos schools. She lives in San Cristobal, New Mexico. Visit her website at www.catherinestrisik.com.

CPSIA information can be obtained
at www.ICGtesting.com
Printed in the USA
FSOW03n1845010616
20927FS